D0794520

Wacky Weather and Silly Season Jokes

Laugh and Learn About Science

Written by Melissa Stewart
Illustrated by Gerald Kelley

ROCK SPRINGS LIBRARY
SWEETWATER COUNTY
ROCK SPRINGS

Enslow Elementary, an imprint of Enslow Publishers, Inc.

Enslow Elementary® is a registered trademark of Enslow Publishers, Inc.

Copyright © 2012 by Melissa Stewart

All rights reserved.

No part of this book may be reproduced by any means without the written permission of the publisher.

Library of Congress Cataloging-in-Publication Data:

Stewart, Melissa.

   Wacky weather and silly season jokes: laugh and learn about science / written by Melissa Stewart ; illustrated by Gerald Kelley.

       p. cm. — (Super silly science jokes)

   Includes index.

   Summary: "Learn about sun, rain, tornadoes, snow, the reason for the seasons, and more. Read jokes about all of these topics, and learn how to write your own"—Provided by publisher.

   ISBN 978-0-7660-3971-1

   1. Weather—Juvenile literature. 2. Seasons—Juvenile literature. 3. Weather—Juvenile humor. 4. Seasons—Juvenile humor. I. Kelley, Gerald. II. Title.

   QC981.3.S738 2012

   551.602'04—dc23

                              2011026531

Future editions:

Paperback ISBN 978-1-4644-0168-8

ePUB ISBN 978-1-4645-1075-5

PDF ISBN 978-1-4645-1075-2

Printed in China

012012 Leo Paper Group, Heshan City, Guangdong, China

10 9 8 7 6 5 4 3 2 1

To Our Readers: We have done our best to make sure all Internet Addresses in this book were active and appropriate when we went to press. However, the author and the publisher have no control over and assume no liability for the material available on those Internet sites or on other Web sites they may link to. Any comments or suggestions can be sent by e-mail to comments@enslow.com or to the address on the back cover.

Illustration Credits: © 2011 Gerald Kelley (www.geraldkelley.com)

Photo Credits: © 2011 Photos.com, a division of Getty Images, pp. 12, 15, 17, 24; AP Images/ The Lawrence Journal-World, Nick Krug, p. 36; Enslow Publishers, Inc., p. 44; FEMA/Michael Rieger, p. 31; iStockphoto.com: © Ales Veluscek, p. 32, © quavondo, p. 18, © wdstock, p. 4; NASA, p. 27; Shutterstock.com, pp. 1, 6, 23, 28, 35, 38, 40, 43; Tom LaBaff and Stephanie LaBaff, pp. 8, 11, 20.

Cover Illustration: © 2011 Gerald Kelley (www.geraldkelley.com)

Enslow Elementary

an imprint of

 Enslow Publishers, Inc.

40 Industrial Road
Box 398
Berkeley Heights, NJ 07922
USA

http://www.enslow.com

Contents

1 What's the Weather?

Is it sunny or rainy right now? Hot or cold?

Of course, you know the answers to these questions. Everybody does. We all pay attention to the weather.

The weather influences what clothes we wear. And it controls how much time we spend outdoors. Sunny weather makes for a perfect picnic. But stormy weather can destroy a town in minutes. That's why we all keep an eye on the sky.

As you read this book, you'll learn all about the weather. But that's not all. This book is also chock full of jokes. Some of them will make you laugh out loud. Others might make you groan. (Sorry!) But either way, you'll have a good time. So let's get started!

Q: Why did the weather ask for privacy?

A: It wanted to change.

DO NOT DISTURB

Q: Why isn't the sky happy on clear, sunny days?

A: It has the blues.

2 Where's the Weather?

The weather is what's happening in the **air** around you right this very minute.

What is air? It's the mixture of gases that surrounds our planet. Those gases form Earth's **atmosphere**.

The atmosphere rises about 100 miles (160 kilometers) into the sky. But all the action is just above our heads. Weather happens in the troposphere—the 10-mile (16-km) layer closest to Earth's surface.

Wondering why? It's because **gravity** tugs on the atmosphere. It pulls almost all of the gases in the atmosphere down into the troposphere. And weather can't happen without those gases.

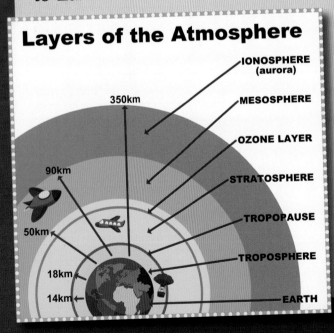

Layers of the Atmosphere

IONOSPHERE (aurora)

350km

MESOSPHERE

OZONE LAYER

90km

STRATOSPHERE

50km

TROPOPAUSE

18km

TROPOSPHERE

14km

EARTH

Q: Why is the Sun glad to be almost 93 million miles (150 million km) away from Earth?

A: Because Earth's atmosphere is so gassy.

Q: Why do large planes spend time flying in both the troposphere and the stratosphere?

A: To be air-fare.

Q: What happened when the atmosphere tried to run away from home?

A: It suddenly understood the gravity of its situation.

3 The Sizzling Sun

Bright sunlight shines down on Earth all day long. The heat energy it gives off warms the water and the land. But some areas of Earth catch more rays than others.

Earth is round, like a ball. That means areas near the **equator** soak up direct sunlight all year long. But warming the **poles** isn't so easy. The Sun's rays have to travel farther through the chilly upper atmosphere. By the time sunlight strikes the top and bottom of the planet, it's lost some of its heat. And that's not all. The heat that's left over is spread thin over a wide area of land and sea. No wonder Vostock, Antarctica, is the coldest place on Earth!

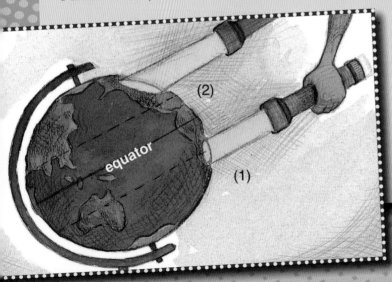

(2)

equator

(1)

See how the light shines over a larger area in the north (2) than it does closer to the equator (1).

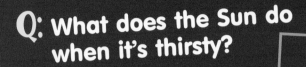

Q: What does the Sun do when it's thirsty?

A: It takes out its sun glasses and melts a few icebergs.

Q: What did the North Pole say to the equator?

A: "You're hot stuff."

4 The Reason for the Seasons

In most parts of the world, weather changes with the **seasons**. That's because Earth is always on the move.

Each year Earth orbits, or makes one complete circle around, the Sun. Different parts of our planet tilt toward the Sun at different points in the **orbit**.

It is summer in places that are tipped toward the Sun. In North America, Europe, and Asia, people enjoy long, warm days in June through August. That's when the northern half of Earth is closest to the Sun.

Areas of Earth that tilt away from the Sun get less heat and light. So the days are short and chilly. In North America, Europe, and Asia, winter comes in December through February.

Q: Why did the penguin visit North America in the winter?

A: So it could chill out.

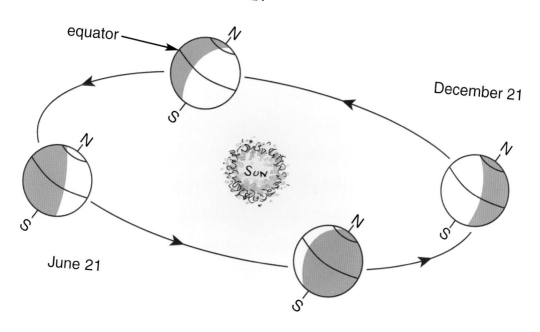

March 21

equator

December 21

SUN

June 21

September 21

Q: Why does Earth move in circles around the Sun?

A: It doesn't want to be square.

5 Air on the Move

Have you ever seen the ocean boil? What about a melting mountain? Of course not! But that's what might happen if Earth's surface held onto all the heat it gets from the Sun.

Luckily, the land and water give off some of their heat energy. It bounces back into the air. And what happens next might surprise you.

When air heats up, it expands. As the air spreads out, it becomes lighter. So it rises up into the atmosphere. At the same time, cooler, heavier air rushes down to take its place. What do we call that moving air? Wind.

Q: Why did the wind finish the test before anyone else in the class?

A: She thought it was a breeze.

Q: Why did the Sun heat up the atmosphere?

A: He wanted the air to lighten up.

Fog, Dew, and Frost

The air around us contains at least a dozen different gases. But when it comes to weather, the most important gas is water vapor. Here's why.

As the sun beats down on lakes and oceans, liquid water heats up and evaporates. It changes into a gas called water vapor and rises into the air.

Warm air can hold more moisture than cool air. So as the temperature falls at night, water vapor cools down and begins to **condense**. The gas changes into tiny droplets of water.

Sometimes millions of water droplets hang in the air close to the ground. We see them as fog. When water vapor condenses on objects like grass, leaves, or spider webs, we see dew. If the night temperature plunges below the freezing point, frost covers the grass.

Q: Why did the water vapor condense?

A: It wanted to dew something.

Q: What does fog like to do on Saturday nights?

A: Just hang around.

7

A Look at Clouds

Have you ever noticed that fog looks a lot like clouds? There's a good reason for that. They're made of the same stuff—tiny water droplets.

During the day, warm air expands. It rises high into the atmosphere. When it bumps into a cooler **air mass**, it loses some of its heat. And you know what that means—its water vapor begins to condense.

What happens to all those itty-bitty drops? They form a cloud.

Scientists divide clouds into three major groups. High, wispy **cirrus clouds** are usually a sign of good weather. Puffy piles of **cumulus clouds** can bring showers. Thick, low layers of **stratus clouds** usually mean a day of heavy rain and drizzle.

Q: What do all three kinds of clouds have in common?

A: The letters "us."

Q: What's the difference between a cloud and a horse?

A: One is reined up and the other rains down.

ROCK SPRINGS LIBRARY
SWEETWATER COUNTY LIBRARY
ROCK SPRINGS

8 Will It Rain?

Inside clouds, water droplets budge, bump, crash, and clump. They grow larger and larger, heavier and heavier, until . . . Hey, hold it! Making rain isn't nearly that simple.

It takes as many as 15 million tiny water droplets to form a raindrop large enough to fall to the earth. That's a whole lot of crashing and clumping. Most clouds just aren't up to the task.

Believe it or not, most clouds never shed a single raindrop. That's right. Just one in every ten clouds showers down on us.

The smallest drops are called drizzle. They're about the size of a pinhead. The largest raindrops are about the size of a pea. They pour down at speeds of up to 20 miles (32 km) per hour.

Q: Why don't mother kangaroos like rainy days?

A: The kids have to play inside.

Q: What falls but never gets hurt?

A: The rain.

9 It's Raining Fish and Frogs

clouds where water condenses

sun

EVAPORATION

rain

OCEAN

The Water Cycle

Ever heard someone say, "It's raining cats and dogs"? That silly saying just means it's raining really hard.

But guess what! Sometimes animals do rain down from the sky. Really. It's true.

It's rained frogs in Japan and fish in Rhode Island. During recess, students in Scotland were showered with worms. And a downpour full of spiders drenched people in Argentina. Yikes!

And guess what else. Nobody knows why or how the little critters got into the sky. Some scientists think strong winds may have lifted the animals up and carried them along. Then, when the winds died down, the animals dropped to the ground. One thing's for sure, fish and frogs aren't a natural part of the **water cycle**.

Q: What happens when it rains cats and dogs?

A: You have to be careful not to step in a poodle.

Q: What goes up when rain comes down?

A: Umbrellas.

Flash and Crash

Sunny. Steamy. Summer. These are just the right conditions for a thunderstorm.

As the first raindrops fall from a **thunderhead**, ice begins to form inside the cloud. Hot and cool air masses swirl together, hurling the icy bits into one another. SMACK! BAM! Each collision makes the cloud more and more electrically charged.

The charge builds and builds until . . . FLASH! Sparks of **electricity** zigzag through the sky.

Each stroke of lightning blasts the air with 50,000 degrees Fahrenheit (28,000 degrees Celsius) of heat energy. That's five times hotter than the surface of the sun. Wow!

As the air surrounding the lightning bolt heats up, it expands very quickly. CRASH! A violent shockwave explodes through the sky, creating the loud crackling crash we call thunder.

Q: Why do raindrops like lightning at night?

A: It helps them see where they're going.

Q: What kind of music does thunder like best?

A: Rock and roll.

Towering Twisters

Spinning, swirling, twisting, twirling—the spiraling winds inside a thunderhead can reach speeds of more than 300 miles (483 km) per hour. And sometimes they take on a life of their own.

It happens about seven hundred times a year in North America. The whirling winds form a funnel-shaped cloud that stretches down to the ground. It's a **tornado**.

The instant a tornado touches down on the ground, dirt and debris explode in every direction. Sometimes the curved cloud settles in one spot. But most of the time, it bounces along at up to 60 miles (97 km) per hour. The twister sucks up everything in its path. It's strong enough to knock down houses, lift cars, and uproot trees.

Q: What's a tornado's favorite game?

A: Twister.

Q: What did the tornado say to the car?

A: "Wanna go for a spin?"

12 Swirling Sea Storms

Imagine a storm that stretches from Chicago, Illinois, to Boston, Massachusetts. Hundreds of thunderheads blast the earth with intense downpours. Day after day, whirlpooling winds whip at 150 miles (250 km) per hour. That's what a **hurricane** is like.

The swirling storms start at sea. When the ocean heats up to 80°F (27°C), huge amounts of water evaporate and rise into the sky. As cooler air rushes down to take its place, whirling winds are set in motion. They spin around a calm center called an eye.

The instant a hurricane hits land, it starts to lose energy. But that first strike can do a lot of damage. Hurricanes wash away beaches. They sink boats. They knock over buildings and topple trees. Hurricanes kill more people than all other storms combined.

Q: Why do hurricanes travel so fast?

A: Because otherwise, they'd be called slow-i-canes.

Q: Why did the hurricane winds stop spinning in circles?

A: They got dizzy.

13 The Story of Snow

Bet you can't guess what Fort Keogh, Montana, is famous for. Give up? The biggest snowflake on record. The giant flake fell on January 28, 1887. It was 15 inches (38 cm) wide. Yowzah!

How did that huge flake form? Just like every other snowflake that's ever dropped from the sky.

In winter, the atmosphere chills out. And so do clouds. Some of their tiny water droplets freeze. Wet droplets stick to the ice, and they freeze too.

As more and more droplets join the party, the ice crystal grows heavier and heavier. Finally, it plunges downward.

As ice crystals fall, they latch onto one another and form snowflakes. By the time a flake hits the ground, it is made of hundreds—or even thousands—of crystals.

Q: What did the cloud say to the ice crystal?

A: "Bon voyage!"

Q: What do snowflakes eat for dessert?

A: Ice cream.

14 Snowflakes and Snowstorms

Every snowflake is different, and so is every snowstorm.

A single storm can blanket the land with millions—maybe even billions—of flakes. And each one is as unique as you are. Still, some flakes do look similar. So scientists group them based on their shapes.

When the air is frigid, snow is dry and powdery. But when the temperature is close to the freezing point, snowflakes are big and wet. This sticky snow is perfect for making snowballs and snowmen.

Some snowstorms deliver just a light dusting. Others dump several feet of snow. Paradise, Washington, may be the snowiest place on Earth. Some years it receives more than 1,000 inches (2,540 cm) of snow. That's enough snow to bury an eight-story building!

Q: Why do scientists measure snowfall in inches?

A: Because snowflakes don't have feet.

Q: What happens when you cross a snowball with a vampire?

A: You get frostbite.

31

All Kinds of Ice

Falling snowflakes have a long trip to the ground. And a lot can happen along the way.

Snow may start to melt on the way down. Or it can mix with rain. The result is sleet.

Freezing rain falls as watery drops. But it freezes the instant it touches the ground. It creates a thin layer of ice called glaze.

You won't see hailstones on cold, winter days. They only form inside summertime thunderheads. Whipping winds sweep water droplets up so high that they freeze. As the ice falls, it begins to melt. But then winds whisk the ice up again. During each upward journey, a new layer of ice coats the hailstone. Large hailstones can have more than twenty icy layers. Wow!

Most hailstones are the size of peas, but some are as large as grapefruits. Large chunks plummet downward at more than 90 miles (145 km) per hour.

Q: What did the hailstone say to the hairdresser?

A: "Give me lots of layers."

Q: Why did the ice crystal panic?

A: It got lost in a glaze maze.

16 The Changing Climate

What is **climate**? Good question. It's the average weather conditions in a place over a period of time.

Weather isn't forever. It changes over time. Twenty thousand years ago, most of North America was covered with ice. Scientists call that period of time the Ice Age. There have been at least five major ice ages since Earth formed.

Right now, our planet is heating up. Why? Because people are changing the atmosphere. We burn oil, coal, and natural gas to heat homes and power cars. That creates **greenhouse gases**. They trap the sun's heat in the atmosphere.

Warmer temperatures can harm other creatures, too. They make plants flower and produce fruit too early. Birds haven't migrated from their winter homes yet. The fruit rots. And when the birds arrive, they starve.

Q: What does a power plant do the night before it has a big test?

A: It burns the midnight oil.

Q: What did mammoths eat during the Ice Age?

A: Snow cones.

17 Weather Watch

What do people talk about more than anything else? The weather. That's because it affects our lives in so many ways.

Too much sun? Crops can die.

Too much wind? Power lines can snap and tumble to the ground.

Too much snow? Hooray! School is cancelled.

We can't control the weather. But scientists called **meteorologists** try to predict it. They monitor weather stations that measure temperature, rainfall, and wind speed and direction. They launch weather balloons to learn about the atmosphere. They track storms using data from weather satellites high above Earth.

Meteorologists watch the weather all day and all night. And if they spot trouble, they let people know right away. Their hard work helps keep us safe.

This scientist launches a weather balloon.

Q: Why did the woman walk outside with her purse wide open?

A: She expected some change in the weather.

Q: What's a meteorologist's favorite day of the week?

A: Sun-day.

How to Write Your Own Jokes

Writing jokes isn't hard if you keep three helpful hints in mind:

1. It's usually easier to think of a joke's punch line, or answer, first. Then work backward to come up with the setup, or question.

2. Keep the setup short and simple. People who listen to your joke will want to try to guess the answer. It's half the fun of hearing the joke. But if the question is too long, your listeners won't be able to remember it all. They'll feel frustrated instead of excited.

3. Keep the answer short and simple too. That way it will pack more of a punch.

Popular Expressions

Ever heard someone say: "I have my *eye* on you"? Maybe it was your mom or your teacher. It means she thought you might try to do something naughty or sneaky. So she was going to watch you carefully.

Can you use this popular expression as the punch line for a joke? You bet!

The calm center of a hurricane is called the *eye*. At some point, it will pass over everything in the sea storm's path. So here's a question that works perfectly with your punch line:

Q: What did the hurricane say to the island?

A: "I have my eye on you."

Can you think of another joke that uses a popular expression as a punch line?

Homographs and Homophones

A homograph is a word with two or more different meanings. One example is the word *dove*. It can refer to a common bird. It is also the brand name of a popular ice cream treat.

You can create a question that seems to use one definition of the word and an answer that uses the other. Here's an example:

Q: Why did the cloud lick its lips?

A: A DoveBar® flew by.

Homophones are two or more words that sound the same, but are spelled differently and have different meanings. For example, the words *fare* and *fair* are homophones.

You can create a great joke by mixing homophones. Here's an example:

Q: Why do large planes spend time flying in both the troposphere and the stratosphere?

A: To be air-fair.

These jokes are fun because your family and friends might be able to guess the answers. And sometimes they'll come up with different answers that are just as good. Then you'll have some brand-new jokes to tell someone else.

You can have lots of fun using homographs and homophones to create jokes that will amuse your friends.

Similar Sounds, Different Meanings

Changing a few little letters can also result in words that sound almost the same, like *climate* and *climb it* or *cheetah* and *cheater*. And these word pairs can be the inspiration for some hilarious jokes.

Here's an example:

Q: **What's the difference between weather and climate?**

A: **You can't weather a tree, but you can climate.**

Can you think of your own weather joke that uses similar-sounding words to really pack a punch?

Ha Ha Ha

He He He

Rhyme Time

Playing with words to create rhymes can be highly entertaining. It's even better when a rhyme is the heart of a joke. Here's an example:

Q: What's it called when a raindrop and a snowflake shake hands?

A: A sleeting greeting.

Getting Silly

Sometimes the best jokes are ones that are just plain silly or ridiculous. Get ready to laugh out loud—here are some great examples:

Q: Why did the tornado cross the playground?

A: To get to the other slide.

Q: What happens when it rains cats and dogs?

A: You hear "Me-ouch" and "Bow-wowch."

Your Jokes in Print

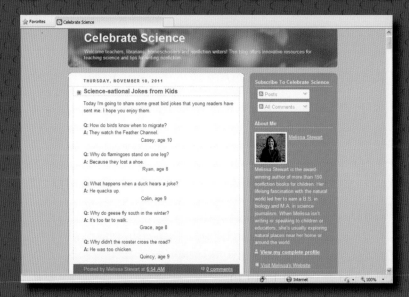

Now it's your turn. See if you can come up with some seriously silly jokes of your own. Then share them with your family and friends.

You can submit your most science-sational jokes to:

mas@melissa-stewart.com.
Be sure to include your first name and your age.

The best jokes will be posted on Fridays at:
http://celebratescience.blogspot.com
People all over the world will be able to read and enjoy them. You can send drawings too. Now get to work on some jokes, and don't forget to have a good time!

Words to Know

air—The collection of gases that make up Earth's atmosphere.

air mass—A cluster of air at a constant temperature. Some air masses are warmer than others.

atmosphere—The layer of gases that surrounds Earth or another body in space.

cirrus cloud—A wispy cloud high in the atmosphere.

climate—The average weather in an area over a period of time.

condense—To change from a gas to a liquid.

cumulus cloud—A puffy cloud that may develop into a thunderhead.

electricity—Energy resulting from the flow of charged particles.

equator—An imaginary line around the middle of Earth. It is halfway between the North Pole and the South Pole.

gravity—The force that pulls objects toward the center of Earth or other body in space.

greenhouse gases—Gases that cause global warming by trapping heat from the Sun in Earth's atmosphere.

hurricane—A destructive tropical storm that forms over warm water and has winds of at least 74 miles (119 km) per hour.

meteorologist—A scientist who studies the weather.

orbit—The path of a body in space as it moves around a larger object with more gravitational pull.

poles—One of the two opposite ends of Earth in relationship to the equator.

season—One of four periods of the year with predictable weather patterns.

stratus cloud—A low, dark cloud that usually occurs in layers.

thunderhead—A cloud that produces a thunderstorm.

tornado—A destructive windstorm that can form over land during a thunderstorm.

water cycle—The never-ending process in which water evaporates, rises into the sky and forms clouds, and then rains or snows to produce more water.

Learn More

Books

Breen, Mark and Kathleen Friestad. *The Kids' Book of Weather Forecasting*. Danbury, Conn.: Ideals Publications, 2008.

Carson, Mary Kay. *Inside Weather*. New York: Sterling, 2011.

Hellweg, Paul. *The American Heritage Children's Thesaurus*. New York: Houghton Mifflin Harcourt, 2007.

Wittells, Harriet and Joan Greisman. *The Clear and Simple Thesaurus Dictionary*. New York: Grosset & Dunlap, 2006.

Internet Addresses

The Weather Channel Kids!

http://www.theweatherchannelkids.com/

Weather Wiz Kids

http://weatherwizkids.com/

Index

39092 08291229 8

SWEET---- ---- ---- LIBRARY SYS
---- ----, WY

SEP 2 1 2012

ROCK SPRINGS LIBRARY

400 C Street

Rock Springs, WY 82901

307 352 6667

RK J 551.6 STEW
39092082912298
STEWART, MELISSA.
WACKY WEATHER AND SILLY
SEASON JOKES